My Own Written Winter

My Own Written Winter

poems by
Jonathan D. Pigno

photographs by
Andrew E. Lisanti III

Copyright © 2017 Jonathan D. Pigno
All rights reserved.

ISBN: 0692869824
ISBN 13: 9780692869826
Library of Congress Control Number: 2017905296
57 Press, Staten Island , NY

For Mom and Dad:

My family
My heart
My reason
My spirit
My purpose
My meaning
My hope
My world.

In memory of Anthony Pigno—
Equal parts special, innocent, unique, and extraordinary.

An uncle, a friend, and an inspiration.

Table of Contents

Prologue · xv

I.   Challenging the Frost · 1
Succulent Ink · 3
Problem Solver · 4
Day of Rest · 5
Chicago · 6
Praying Hands · 9
I Can't Stay · 11
Steady Paradox · 15
Doubting Thomas · 16
Conditional · 19
Battery Acid · 21
Preservative · 22
Keep Trying · 24
Chip off the Old Buck · 26
Took a Break (Bad Idea) · 28
Weight in Salt · 30
He Was Gifted · 32
Snakeskin · 35
Trespassing · 37
Standard Response · 39
Plot of Choice · 41

Matter of Trust · 43
Breakfast · 45
Daily Special · 47
Off-Road · 48
Dear Anthony · 50
Begrudgingly · 52
Got What You Came For · 54
On Exhibit · 56
Whore for the Establishment · 59
Proven Not Published · 61
Hold Our Own · 63
Lint Roller · 65
Teetotaler · 68

II. Voices Etched in Ice · 71
Sleep (Noose) · 73
Lack of Confidence · 74
Evolution (Isn't Straight) · 75
Turntable · 76
D. · 78
Four Years Ago · 80
Blurred Vision · 81
Valet Park (My Heart) · 82
Post–Manic Pixie Syndrome (Part 2) · · · · · · · · · · · · · · 85
Play Set · 88
Family Album · 90
Can't Put It into Words · 91
At Your Door · 93
Go Get Help—I Think He Fell Down the Well · · · · · · 95
Enjoy Your Golden Years · 98
November Parkway · 99
Weekend in Her Sun · 101

Arden Avenue · 103
Ballad of the Linen Closet · 108
Better Son · 112

III.   White and Blurring Lines · 113
Act of God · 115
A Worthless Attempt · 116
Sappho · 118
Cosmic Light Unknown · 119
Don't Blame the Messenger · 120
Size Never Mattered · 121
Word Bitten · 122
Daily Nothing · 123
Always a Perfectionist (Magician) · · · · · · · · · · · · · · · · · · 124
Gnosis · 126
True and Just · 127
Retrospective (Integer) · 129
Checkerboard · 131
Robin's Nest (Never You) · 134
New Face · 137
Rail Yard (The Switchman) · 139
Almost Lost the War · 143
Commitment · 147
Silk Flowers · 149
They Wear T-Shirts · 151
Transit Lane · 153
Waiting Area · 155

IV.   This Blank and Frozen Slate · 157
Flew the Coop · 159
A Series of Dots · 160
Maya · 162

Young and Naive · 164
Woman of the Sky · 167
Toujours · 169
Mother of Exploration · · · · · · · · · · · · · · · · · 171
A Night Away · 173
Fresh Start · 175
Village Winter · 177
Joyce at One a.m. · 178
Timekeeper · 182
Why It Goes Unsaid · · · · · · · · · · · · · · · · · · 185
Reader · 187
Source · 189
A Type of Poetic Justice · · · · · · · · · · · · · · · 191
Point of Entry · 193
Rest Assured · 197
Composition · 199

V. Skating across the Cracks · · · · · · · · · · 201
Outpatient Therapy · · · · · · · · · · · · · · · · · · · 203
Made an Attempt · 203
Can't Say You Didn't · · · · · · · · · · · · · · · · · · 204
Truth Hurts · 204
Hasty Decision · 205
Kept to Oneself · 205
Two Sides · 206
Contrived · 207
Embellished · 207
OCD · 208
Borderline · 208
Bad Couple of Weeks · · · · · · · · · · · · · · · · · · 209
Says a Lot about Me · · · · · · · · · · · · · · · · · · · 210
Contract · 210

Indulgence	211
Author's Rope	211
Back and Forth	212
Cup of Coffee	212
Self-Employed (Salary)	213
Man of Many Words	214
Burden	214
Pharisee	215
Feigning Confidence	216
No Apologies	216
Perpetual	217
Can't Win 'Em All	218
Here Comes the End	218
Advice to My Father	220
Fleeting Thought	220
Sour Grapes	221
Chewed Out	221
All the Trouble I'd Save	222
Give Thanks	223
Last-Ditch Effort	223
Chokehold	224
Some Reason, Some Season	225
Acknowledgments	227
About the Author	229

Prologue

This blizzard is a stifling tempest that I just can't seem to suffer, as it hails from the cruelest ambitions in the depths of impossible dreams—clouds that scatter the ether of my appetites known for resistance, far and wide skies of displeasure abusing this gift to endure.

For my heart seeks its rarest desire to get lost in the white of these trees, to wander with polar discretion among intentions that are best left unsure—a persistent but selfless vocation that is blank as the slate of this winter, where the branches of my words are a fixture on the canvas of voices in snow.

Where wilderness houses my miseries, my ghosts, and shattered fulfillments as unique but separate reminders made in equal measures of hurt—a place built of quiet confessions and exposures by silence in frigidness, a whisper of losses among breezes that bear life in the kiss of their frost.

It is a challenge to the climates so bitter their wars are a temperature dropping to the point where all hate is an avalanche that echoes in forgiveness alone.

It's a hush in the lull of a creation, a ballad of the voice with no reason other than to state its objective as a beautiful but idle relief—in expression where rage is depicted as a flake on a window that's melting, showing each curve of said miracle as it fades in the breath that I've lost.

It's a crack of the mind at its weakest and a plea of innocence grieving for the empty slate to bear witness to what freedom is guilty as charged.

It is from here I draw inspiration.

It is in failure that each writer is born and renewed like earth every season so that creation trumps all with its will.

So follow this path into reticence, where the lines are isolation explored and exchanges of hope in such blurriness for proof of what spring that's to come—an amalgam of truths that are meaningless as the fury of spite in my rambling that translates to love if you'd let it when listening for the me that is there.

I.
Challenging the Frost

Succulent Ink

To write
Is to savor
Rejection
On the forlorn palette
Of hope
As you conquer
This verbal addiction
With hunger
For the flagrant taste
Of art
In spite of the critic
Whose recipe
Is added salt.

Problem Solver

I'm the fracture
Beneath your heel
A wanton
Son of grace
Who treads
The steep imbalance
While remaining
Inclined to sin
As I'm trampled
Underfoot
Brittle
Like aging bone
Suffering
With due cause
This pain
Of broken chance.

Day of Rest

I owe myself
This pleasure
Of undue
And misaligned idleness
The gluttonous
And painstaking hour
A tedious
And carnal measure
Of thumbs
Twiddled like ice picks
Conundrums
Cutting the veil
Angled
To chisel at will
And in paradox
Be a steady cause
To the wry
And sarcastic suggestion
That I am a person
Of worthiness
Whose sentence
Is the fruit
Of toil
And verbosity
A product of meaning.

Chicago

It's been
Too many years
Since she first
Appeared in my dreams
And offered
The kind of solace
I'd expected
Only from God

At first
I thought her an angel
So enlightened
So carelessly bold

But soon
I acknowledged a vision
A muse
An image
A girl

I could only
Call her Mia—
A savior of my own—
The one who kissed
My wounds
The woman who slept
In my sheets
Figuratively

In my heart
And showed me
The promise of faith
And the healing
Potential of love
As I imagine
Her porcelain face
With bangs
And bobbing hair
Peach
Like a summer spell
And with flowers
A revelation
Crown atop her head
The liberation
Of my soul
In her eyes
The widening field
Of a lifetime
United in Christ
And the freedom
To explore creation
And live impulsively
By the whole
Through beauty
In art made flesh.

Now I'm a tired man
With women
Who've come and gone
But still
I smell her essence

And breathe
The passion in name
As I wonder
If I'm a lunatic
To follow
Where I'd envisioned
Like the narrative
Of my life
Awaiting its timely play
And the epilogue
Of coming nightmares
All beginning
With pleasant dreams
At her feet
Where I still worship
The bride that wasn't there
But in me
All along.

I guess
I'm going
To Chicago.

I need
To know
She's real.

Praying Hands

The tattoo
On your wrist
Is not a favor
Of God
Or an emblem
On your arm
To vindicate
Countless sins
That compel
The suffering arrogant
As they squander
The gift of intellect
For the quick
And futile trade-off
Of brawn
Bravery
And strength
In all the wrong
Festering halos
On the shoulders
Of faithless men
As those
Who delight in embers
To be burned
In comforting hell
Or emptiness
On which they prosper
By the flex

Of similar muscle
Inscribed with praying hands
But surrounded
By evil tongues

For the hypocrites
To always see
And likewise
To be appalled
But for ink
To bleed in waste
As it tells
Of a simple wrong.

I Can't Stay

To choke
On the curse of words
Is to swing
From the noose of God
And question
The unseen hardships
Of trivialities
Best explored

I ask myself
Every morning
As breath
Escapes my tantrum
From a voice
In panicked reason
On a bed
Of sweat and terror
How the transient
And unfortunate mystery
Became the visible
And tangible star
Of an orbit
Lacking reason
Or some other
Explainable origin
As I listen
To the voice of others
Mingling day to day

Processing their inward doubts
But denying all outward cause
And commuting
On the rails of monotony
One existential folly
At a clip—

I think
There must be
An issue

Or I truly
Wish
I were dead

Because then
I'd have my answer
As to how this
Remains accepted
When I've tried
So hard to achieve
But in its place
Is always
The words:

The compulsion
The art
The reckoning

Not money
Or love
Or friendship

Just the ranting
And desperate phrase
Of a philosopher
In need of a bullet
Or a good enough
Reason to work
And an excuse
To avoid the laughter
Of men
Who think better of drudgery
And women
Who deny their complicity
In attempts
To diminish my worth
And idolize
A hero of muscle
Instead of that guy
Who talks pretty
And thinks so much
That it hurts

It's OK
'Cause you know
I hate myself

I excel
At all costs
Where it counts

And now come
The words
With their doubts

As I struggle
To maintain a semblance
Of life
In the wake of ink
An aggressive
Or awkward phrase
Of needier
And crazier terms
Unheard
By relatable voicelessness
Till some point
When the pen runs out
Soon
I'll give nothing
Back

I can't work
I can't fuck
I can't stay

Let me leave
Let me write
Let me end.

Steady Paradox

I fear being able
To balance
The steady
And unending paradox
Of surviving
While remaining creative
In the relentless
Outcome of trials
Suited
To the will of liars
And moneymakers
Alive and well
Contradicting
Their entire whole
While preserving
Part of themselves
To prosper
Idle
And perish
From the gaze
Of richer kings
Whose dominion
Is the casting die
And war
Just a peacekeeping toy.

Doubting Thomas

This suit
Is a perfect fit—
Pin and needle couture
For the burial
Of every sentiment
I'd imagined
In the throngs of pleasure
Every romance
I've carried in prose
Every destiny
I squandered in favor
Of a life
Assuredly wasted
By virtue of dreams
So dull

Crucified
Now in adulthood
As the teen
Remembers apathy
And the college student
Recalls fruitless knowledge
But the man
Forgets poetic ideals
As he scrambles
To preserve his dreams
Dressed in formal attire
As the stake

Is driven through wood
And the muse
Bleeds out on Calvary
Near the mount
Where Christ was questioned

It is similar
Nonetheless
Like the swarm
Of our devious ills
To the ways
We forget our love
Or beauty
In heavy-handed judgment
Of flesh
Or the acted gospel
Of expectation
Whether right or wrong

Self-righteousness
Self-imposed
By the critic
Who conquers the child
And the wallet
Who suckles its monster
At the teat
Of necessary invention
Like a birth
Of accepted devils
Whose sole purpose
Is to harm our life
With the humdrum

Monotonous
And calculated
Measured at will
To a T

So tell me
You believe
In artistry

I'll show you
A resurrected Savior

'Cause forever
From now
Is Golgotha

And the skull
On my chest
Is hope

As far as any God
Could be
With the doubts of Thomas
In mind
And the plague of ink
As my prayer
When the cold of hell
Tricks my soul.

Conditional

I never
Would have thought
I'd be the one
Wasting breath
Fearful
Of standing silent
And walking
From idle comforts
As the mass
Of dwindling favor
Weighs heavy
On certain hearts
Occupies
Familial need
But becomes
The gaseous state
Of expectedness
Soon evaporated
Into hurt
Like transient air

Taken through
Moving lungs
As a symbol
Of what's still breathing
Inward

Through that path
And out
From a closing passage

Gagging
On conditional favor
Like love
That has us running

From the ambivalence
Of death and fumes
Asphyxiation
By common threats
And suffocating
Under roofs
Singular
But not removed

Home
Is an empty space

Our lives
a lingering smoke.

Battery Acid

We leaked
And covered our faults
As alkali
Coated our nerves
And energy once stored
Exploded
In attempt to challenge the spillage
And in shock
Grow a positive charge
Negative
As we'd become
But manufactured
To produce a spark
And burst
With a proper sendoff
Depleting what's left
Of our usage
To die
When the time was right.

Preservative

Let's be frivolous
Bold and pale
Shallow and callous
Wrecked
From the wringing of hands
In waiting
And the stopping of clocks
In service
By pretending
The silence is mutual
And testing
Our feelings to death
Like a well-oiled
And effortless cog
Drenched to the brass
In deceit
Fearing the rust
Of rain
As anger
Is our favorite climate
And time
A weather for birds
That hang over
Dustier earths
And promise
The famished moment
With potential
And nourishing gray

Before leaving
To exploit the sun
Without ever pursuing
Its tease
Or providing the land
With its needs
Before streams
Are soaked up
By the ground—
What a waste
To seek love
In this drought
While preserving
But the slightest of drops.

Keep Trying

Every muscle
Tendon
And ligament
Is pulling outward
From a central point
Screaming
In thinning tensions
And tightening
Like clustered knots
To reiterate
The closing of eyelids
And paling of skin
On my face
The soreness
Of standing knees
And frailty
Of jittering hands
That tell
Of a limited effort
In a cycle
With endless curves
And cues
Of constant ailing
For the tasks
That beckon once more
Again
To the frills of exhaustion
Till the kingdom

Of tomorrow has come
And the fallen potential
Is frayed
From the eating away
Of excitement
In the roundabout
Of laboring victims
Or mundane
Causes of love.

Chip off the Old Buck

Hank
Would always mention
To find
Your deepest passion
And let it
Overtake you

To claim you
Until death.

It was easy
For him to say
'Cause the words
Already had.

He had nothing
Left to mention
But the ache
Of empty space

The echo
Of spoken ink
And abuse
Of hollow sound.

Now I know this
Very well
For I too have been
Consumed

And failed as
A so-called writer

A poet
A son
And man

A lover
Believer
And teacher

Worker
Mentor
And friend.

But still I
Turn these terms
As easy as taking breath
And feel like
Instant fire
In the pyre
Of a wooden husk
As it burns
To a mounting inferno
Where the demons
I hide
Can't question
Why I ever bothered
To avoid them
When agony
Was the only way.

Took a Break (Bad Idea)

Remind me
Never to idle
And walk away from
The anxious need
To spit
And conjure fire
From truth
That's called to suffer
Verbosity
Like spoken whips
And lashes
Of rational minds
As I intend
To lose my cool
Or offend
Each possible task
Denounce
The ranks of trying
And call out
The proper nouns
In the stutter
Of hateful opposites
And the ignorance
Of tortured grace
To narrate
Expel
And exercise
The failure of anxious sinners

In communion
By mocking elders
Cursing a respected few
And binging
On spited majorities
So the poet doesn't lose
His vacuum
Of manic and voiceless suction
So corrupted
By the will of dust
Harbored
In brilliant distance
Farthest from
Form or pretense
But prescribed
Like the fuck of days
And hours
Compelled to nothing
As it leaks
Through a pocket of pages
And mocks
The fallacy of readership
Before an audience
Has learned his weakness
Or message
To be ill
And unknown.

Weight in Salt

Let me write
Something substantial
A doubtful
And unwilling confession
Like a lyric
Of furious letdowns
Or a hymn
Of golden restraints
In the lifetime
Of mounting concessions
Dying to the beat
Of acceptance
But living
To the doubtful captives
Who found worth
In the stones
Of their killers
And created
A shrine in their place
Only to learn prayer
Was the difference

Animated
In cruel obsession
But confined
To the page of its word

And carried out
In minds of believers

But built
Like a grotto of man
In salt
By the value of poetry
To the castoffs
Delirious and told

But somehow
Important in structure
As it flows
From one nerve
To the next
And rests
On the anxious balance
Of knowing
Such prose is absurd

This is the need
For literature
No different than zeal
Or religion
No better than magic
To cynics
Or enigmas
Of science unknown

Marvel
At beautiful
Nothing.

Now give me
That round
Of applause.

He Was Gifted

Long have I failed
To apologize
For the string
Of delirious raids
And contemplated acts
Of defiance
I've enacted
On behalf of illness
Or the inspired
High of failure
Or pleasure
Of misused verbs
I've unhinged
Like a broken door
Or busted
Like withered planks
Tethered with spoken nails
And the baggage
Of driven stakes
Like volumes
Of stolen hours
I'd borrowed
From the will of God
And neglected
In abusive terms
Through the lies
In which I've carried
And managed

Like a virtuous journey
From which I'd hoped
To return
But never relive
Or excuse
As a witness
With written genius
Of events defying description
At length
In a changing world;

For this ink
Of parrying destinies
And reliance
On a tired phrase
Is the lasting sack
Of testaments
Obscured
By the merchant's shelf
And concealed
In truthful sands
Far from its truer home
Like leather
Hardbound and weathered
But traded
In a scam of mercy
To maintain
Or make use of loss
That appeals
To the love of phobias
And relishes
In anxious pride

When they say
I was truly gifted
But in reality
Was something less.

Snakeskin

Most disconcerting of all
Is how we shed
Our thickest truths
In the loss
Of realized selves
Through the actual
And humbling threat
Of displacing
Known realities
For the weaker
But deepest fangs
To emerge like
Charred remains
From the mouths
Of screaming cinders
And tongues
Of jealous flames
That light
The bottomless well
For the path
Of mistaken snakes
Unwilling
As they grovel
Slither
Beneath their load
And burdens
Of enticing fear
And the toxin

Of loathsome gods
Who forged
Their unsightly shapes
In the attempt
To make mammals grand
But in turn
Just held a mirror
To the chapped
And chafing remains
Itching with crawling pride
And the image
Of scaled reflections
Of what reptilian
Traits await
Beneath the layers
Of fragile souls
Just as we
Come of age
And learn
To abandon skins
On the grounds
On which we sneak.

Trespassing

Let me ransack
Your perceptions
And unlatch
The narrow locks
That prevent your
Honest discretion
To perceive me
As I am
Not as words entail
Behind walls
Of said disturbance
And the silence
Of stirring grins
In memory
Of who I'm not
And the digging
Of what I was
To excavate
Your death
In hopes
Of eternal insults
That dwell
Beyond expectation
And haunt
Deliberate days
Or possess
Revolving fears
Of becoming

Just like me
As the one who
Trespassed thoughts:

An ideal
To be mocked and maimed
By the ones who said
They love you
And professions assumed
Fulfilling
While pouring dirt
On stone
Now voiceless at the sight
Of a stomped
And unmarked grave
That leaves this truth
Suspended
Between earth
And restless hell.

Standard Response

Dear unwilling applicant
We regret
To delightfully inform you
Your will
And unabashed openness
Indicates utter disdain
For the insanity
Of routine labor
Failure to wholly commit
And a passion
For reckless pleading
To a god
Who shouldn't exist

Because we effectively rendered
Meaning
A useless goal
Of faith
Or creative nonsense
And breath
A valued utility

And your life
A secondary pleasure
The instant
You sent that letter
And knew
Such slavery inevitable

As the onlookers
Are eager to gaze
And judge harshly
While you belabor
The inevitable choice
To ponder
Or eventually yield
To its pressure
And unequivocally
Or wholly
Accept.

Plot of Choice

The older we become
The harder to understand
Or rationalize unequivocally
The permanence of transition
Or perpetual deeds of consequence
And distinguish uneasy heroes
From the goodwill of such villains
And their unintentional choice
By method of adaptation
And cruel faith of survival
As they linger in mud and legacy
And dirt that packs their judgment
From assuming settled ground
Is the only patch of soil
Moist enough to dwell
Descend or idly occupy
Once death has sheathed their pleasures
Or eyes ignore the cash flow
That trickles like excess rain
To the roots beneath their sleep
And supplies them even in absence
With the fortune of fellow men

Like religion buried and damp
But trodden by marching sinners
Whose earth is nearly the same
Whose sky is nearly as dull

Allow me to choose my end
Without feeling my pockets first
Or imbuing the last ones left
With the sense of silver linings

Matter of Trust

Allow me this
Brandished attempt
As a gesture
Of fleeting triumphs
And an artifact
Of defeated worth
So keen
To devalue gifts
And intent
On empowering losses
As the variables
Of fickle readership
Or the shadow
Of this maddening birthright
Obstructed
By the wealth of giants
And vested
In the power of phrase
Long after hindsight
Has fallen
And antiquity has become
Their grace
When the winner
Can barely see
Or perhaps even live
In the moment
When the now
Has become their then—

What a wounded
And vulnerable instance
Or chore to become
My bane
As this pen
Teeters lightly on secrets
But the heart
Demands exhibition
Of blood

All verse
Is a matter
Of trust
Hidden in veins
Of hurt.

Breakfast

A servant I remain
In secret
For the Lord of Words
Bowing my heart
In reverence
And wringing the sinner's rag
By disgrace
I've accrued in neglect
Through a pen
Of countless fallen
In the house
Of open windows
Over talks
And sunny mornings
From the time
I bow my head
And await
The sweetened crust
Or pie and proverbial syrups
With flowers
On quilted linens

Sugar in steaming glasses
Or glimmers
From broken china
That leak
A resistant sunlight
As it turns
In unsteady hands

From the palm
Of a carried mother
Toward the window
In reflection
Or refraction
Of the love of God
So spoiled
And bright to the touch
But coddled
By the lace of curtain
As the matriarch
Brings wealth to the table
And Father
Makes food from toil
And the rest of me
Believes in silence

As if pretending
To be a child
Preoccupied
By this circumstance
As an excuse
To skip my breakfast
Or acknowledge
I'm merely alone
But in turn
A sibling of Christ
Or saint in rejection
Of purpose
Who deliberately
Chooses his destiny
With anything other
Than faith.

Daily Special

I can count by dulling knives
How my friends have cooked
To the grind of wasted tastes
Or blandness of simmering needs
The chopping block of passions
Or blender of expectations
Like a meal or steady performance
Assumed by demanding hosts
And patrons just as ravenous
To savor the juice of self
Identities come to boil
Products kneaded and shaped
Willingly served on platters
Refused on finest china
As cuisine becomes synonymous
With the loss of natural flavor
Or lack of personal flair
From the minds of simple chefs
Like them, a followed recipe
Like me, a burning stove.

Off-Road

No I may never
Be Dean
Or have Sal's
Immortal scroll
But instead
Seek paradise wandered
In the lanes
Of vacant memory
I'd crossed
Like dividing lines
In the dance
Of poetic extremes
In the lunacy
Of immortal threads
Words so
Dangerously conjured
As vanity
Or beloved demons
Goddesses
But common whores
And street lamps
Bright like sparklers
We've seen
During summer blackouts
Dancing through hottest nights
On the porch
With a shimmering radiance

As forgiveness
Of forever worlds
Long lost to cares
We'd thrown
In terms
Like a gunpowder sentence
By poets
So rottenly spastic
Their sins become
Painful jazz
And convulse through dark
Like stars
While the day brings
Clearest abandon
Free as this call
To artistry
Or arms
Of illustrious theft
As the inspired zeal
Of dreamers
Who immortalize
Truth of friends
And turn them
Into golden tales
Before abandon
Has lost its relevance
And disregard
Becomes too frequent
For the inspired turn
Of visionaries
Unafraid
To veer off-road.

Dear Anthony

Maybe
We're not so different
How we tear up the bride
In her garden
And desecrate
This ivory trellis
By digging ourselves
A hole
Deepened
By pride in nothing
Or reasons
Thought too unsettling
To speculate
In staunch realities
As doubters
Of the happy home.

Maybe
We just agree
In the effort it apparently takes
Our whims to be known
As divisive
But easily expressed
As fear
And in hate
Breach the orbit of nervousness
As we ride its tilt
With abandon

And trip on the cracks
In our getaway
Worshipping the scrape
Of that fall

Yes
It's an unsettling pleasure
To destroy
What property
You're given

No
It's a saddening intimacy
To call it a day
When we don't.

Begrudgingly

There's a fine line
Between my poetry
And the ravings of some sickness
For I'm starting
To the think the latter
Is as hopeful as it gets
As this grace of embittered angels
Is hell-bent on such reckoning
Bearing the verbal martyrdom
Of lunatics who can spell
My gift of laughing judgment
My betrayal of honest genius
To appear as sainted conqueror
Against idols of spoken steel

To women
A mess of beauty

To parents
The angry dreamer

To teachers
A grade outclassed

And winners
A loser's victor

I'm a failure and a demon
A lover and lavish peasant
Arrogant but never boring
Beyond your measured worth

I'm valueless and demeaning
Offensive and revered
A madman or a messenger
Because there is no in-between.

Got What You Came For

I'm unafraid
Yet restless
'Cause normalcy can kill
When every dollar bill
Is worth a hundred extra
Or a stake up someone's rear
Could mean
A thousand more

This shallow breath
Of meaning
This tasteless wealth
Of virtue
As coveted imbalance
Like the talk of clearing airs
A release of sacred incense
Up in smoke with vapid mist
Or souls
With scentless willingness
To be sexless in their sense
Distancing their grace
In the billows of their reason
Or arguing their case
In the court of angry gods

By the time
The players realize
There is little they could win

Or defend against the agony
Of absence with a name
Of blackness with no cause
Except maybe
The ones we make
The ones I try to write
And by ink
Prescribe them value
In disdain by anxious words
To obliterate their faith
And find Christ among the ruins
Just before success
Erects its pillared hell
In rubble and in rage
In the hope of bitter fantasy
To wish for existing angels
And rest
By sanctioned grief
Imagining their sleep
Is safe and sound in sin
But ignorant by their law
To know their bed
Is made
And wish for further fortunes
Pleading with abundance
To enjoy it
While it lasts.

On Exhibit

If I fail
To treat you well
It's because it's
Part of the show
And a process
Of contracting lies
By the conundrum
That I swear
Isn't jealousy
But guilty ease
And burden
By falling to pieces
In complicit
And deliberate attitudes
I've created to
Pad these lines

And through bloodletting
Swear these words
Are a mockery
Of such faith
In believing
What kind of man
Could ever allow
His promise
To become
A turn of verse
And in rhythm

A reckless stance
To awake his paling virtue
And engage
A lover's distance
Knowing full well
He's the mouthpiece
The ventriloquist
And knot of strings
To maintain
The puppet's entrance
And invite
A crowd of dolls
To perceive his
Fractured goodness
Or a wooden dance
In haste
In effort to scramble value
And enliven
This sudden image
Like a curator
Gauge its worth
By the wonder
Of such history
Faking knowledge
And fudging mastery
As he hangs
On the walls like paintings
And swings
From the gallery loft
To escape the coming judgment
Of those
Who see past his symbol

His folly
His broken oath

For the applause
He had won in his act

From the noose
They call an exhibit

I'm sorry
You were part
Of the cast.

We're all
Casualties
Of the biz.

Whore for the Establishment

I merely see value in maniacs
In derelicts
And heretical nothings
In losers
The passionate artful
In their rabble-rousing intellects
In radicals with colored hair
And saints of inspired defiance
Against the grain
In religious madness
In disclosure
And neurotic truths
Paranoid
Unwillingly hopeful
Faithful
Fatalistic
And zealous
Devout to a certain ends
But culpable through indifference
Honest in lacking meaning
And through sanity
Drawing lines
Between peace and feared confessions
As an agony
Of labor-filled mystery
Hung on the cross of flesh
Donned in the callous streets
And knelt to in empty slums

Down lanes and paper alleys
Interrupted through
Childhood memory
Or violation of angry souls
Wanton in their worship
To relinquish
And restore the goddess
To reclaim that disbelief
Beyond this staunch abandon
At the expense of
Appearing wholesome
Or in wisdom
Supplying tension
With the needed fuck
Of convention
And the poke
From society's length
As a stretch
In the bed
Of harassment
Where we can only
Refuse
To perform.

If we are
The living whores
Then society
Is a dying john.

Proven Not Published

In order
To be a writer
You have to be
Willing to break

I'm here
To tell you
I've broken
And I love
Every fucking minute

All the lines
And senseless ravings
On this verbal
Canvas of scribbles

Each tangled
And spiraled phrasing
With a tattered semblance
At best

Of the edges
Like mental notebooks
Just waiting
For desecration
By graffiti
Of hyper awareness
That taps into

Utter disdain
For the deep
But delicious issues
That allow for an image
So telling

As powerful
As hurt that rears it
From years
Of apparent misuse

So here is my
Worthless gift
Wound tight
In an ugly bow

Find me
A reason
For sharing
As I go
And write you
A book.

Hold Our Own

We all live
To be acknowledged
And ransack
A stash of feeling
Hidden in incentive
Fearless and endangered
Reckless and overused
Vengeful on our knees
And potent
To the extent
Of the instinct
That holds us back
Saps us
Like its venom
And propels us
Subtly forward
By the hate that leaves us
Wanting
And blackened like a space
In the vacuum
Well below us
Or the skyline
Across our hearts
Sucking the raw ambition
To feed a newborn few
By the slaughter
Of so many
By the justice

Of its mess
And in devotion
Finds us waiting
For the Christ
That never came
But sold us
His bestseller
And crashed
The plane of gospel
To sell
A few more copies
Or in authorship
Call it faithfulness
As the rest of us
Hold our bile
Trace our poison
And face our twists

Lick our fate
And call it ugly

Believe each word
And take it home

Teach our children
Claim it's learning

Kiss the book
And hold our own.

Lint Roller

I'd leave you high and dry
And enjoy each hurtful turn
Until the spoken instant
I'd experience sudden knowing
Closure
Staunch exposure
An epiphany of unreality
And spit the final poison
Like a cause
Of perfumed sorrow
I'd bottled in my madness
Potent
Heady
Spoiled
Settled through its words
And prepared my longest hour
Of pristine and manic verse
But found instead through mourning
By the heat of empty sheets
With the mark of sitting ghosts
Their indent
Their fatal poetry
Their soliloquies of faded means
Where I ready myself for heartache
And bleed these aching leads
To unleash a dreamed resentment
My charm of boyish lust
The demand for mother's attention

Or god between your legs
Just how I envisioned
And demand when we're alone
Someway I define you
Somehow I let it win
So poignant
Sullen
And clear
Derivative
In my code

But it's something that you earn
It's work
And made deserved
A load to be carried and spent
Figuratively, beyond the bedroom
And in it, one literal cost
Terms for the unbecoming
A sentence of approaching death
A verdict well bestowed

Such is the curse of beauty
Capable
In steady hands
Or pens, if nature has it
As a twist of what's unsure
And defined by fickle ethics
Religion
Or better men
To be burdened by its end
And a victim of its abandon
In the wisdom of swelling chests

And mystery of such feeling
To grow in artful martyrdom
To plead with righteous loss.

Teetotaler

People find certain joy
In diminishing
Those who persist
Regardless
Of zealous gospel
Or the struggle to be whole
Distinguished
And poised in betterment
Despite what taste
Or eloquence
Creed
And denial of tendency
Is the truth they shame as dull

As they sip
All human decency
By fire from their glass
And turn it back
Like mirrors
With an image
Blurred by wine
Obscured with running streaks
In a faceless haze
Of heroes
Slaves to a certain spirit
That erodes
Such art in waste
Of a talent

Stalling fate
By the miracle
That is stagnant
By delirious
Drip of alcohol
Into veins
For a hopeless thrill.

II.
Voices Etched in Ice

Sleep (Noose)

With each dream
Comes another memory
A subsequent
And remembered death
That strangles
The best of moments
And captures
The taste of loss
As I dangle
Without love
Or purpose
And swing breathlessly
Alone.

Lack of Confidence

I'll write
This perfect epitaph
Of goodwill
And shallow intent
That translates
A latent value
Of laziness
Bought and forgiven
With attitude
Forged in arson
Complacent
As youthful angst
Endangered
As liability
Through flames
Sweeping the distance
And pens weeping
For cause
In the agony
Of falling rafters
Smothered
Beneath their heaviness
As I'm confident
In remaining
Unknown.

Evolution (Isn't Straight)

I spent
Each misused moment
Of my battered
And so-called youth
In prescribing
A tasteless apathy
To make love
To erected walls
Garnered with fists
Of brilliance
By bullies
Whose name was uncertain
Only grunted
Like miserable sins
As the women bruised
My ego
Whispering
While they left me
One dateless night
At a time.

Turntable

My quest
To counterbalance
And offset
The tilted whirl
Of a devotion
Spun and contrived
Is the axis
Of a painful memory
I circle
To conjure melody
And in sound
Become an entry
Of begging
By which I return
To the past
And right my wrongs
In lyrics
As I remain unturned
By your hands
Caressing and warm
And my face
In your sweaty thighs
Rotated
Isolated
And needled
But somehow
Still fulfilling
Warning me

Of coming noise
By the hiss
Of pressing disaster
In the crackle
Of a broken tip.

D.

I can't imagine the absence
Or sense
Of sweetest memory
You created
In the loss of guidance
And the fallout
Of fractured youth

I'm sorry
I even tried
And at times
Abused or insulted
The image
And upheld legacy
Of a man
Worth more than my own

Here's to
A proven mistake
And the prided deceit
Of my words
The hurtful turn
Of my lies
And nauseous guilt
Of idleness
I pitted

In constant complaints
To hide
My jealous projection

Know
There was
Really love

Know that I had
Respect

And in hindsight
Forgive my
Sharpness

As this sin
Has dulled
My edge.

Four Years Ago

I believe you still
To be sick
Even though
I carry the illness
And actualize
The hole of repentance
That falls through my bed
Like a dream
And with phantoms
Of summers long distant
Crept into sheets
As a breeze
And carried your message
Closely
As I dreamt of guilt
Overwhelming
And the June
I began this descent
Into long
And imminent death.

Blurred Vision

It's a privilege
To bury these ashes
In the same place
You said I'd be slaved
From blindness
Or prideful willingness
To be snared
For prettier dreams
Or the lie
Of elusive hopes
And the value
Of solid tomorrows
Obscured
By the vapor of you
Gone *poof*
In meaningless instants

Funny how they fizzle
And fade
And flee
Their potential deviance
As remainders stick
And scar
The expression of a coarser now
To smooth
The gruesome truths
That are yesterdays
Sneaking behind.

Valet Park (My Heart)

The giveaways
Never spoiled much
In the fault of our
Rambling nerves
Except the starlight
In your hair
The streetlight
In my eyes
Philosophy
In our stare
And theory
On sweated palms
As a tale of whimsy told
And dwindled
Like a storybook feeling
And became
A summertime meaning
Or gospel
In your hands
And religion
Like thinning ropes
Cutaway
Gripping
And taut
With truth
At the falling end
As God hung
In a mason jar

And dangled
Like a whizzing firefly
Burned
In a paling moonlight
Before martyrs
And the sainted reckless
Spoke like
Derivative poets
And came
From the widening parking lots
To traverse
The evening shallows
Of August
And shimmering rainfall
Spotted
And thundering clouds
Overhanging
A piece of our park
And wondering
If the season would boil
Without remembering
A single moment
Of the crackling sparklers
That fade
And the echoes
Of covered graffiti
Came through walls
Like coarsest sands
And resounded
A blistering curve
Of the turns
And perfect tantrums

She gave me
In the worst of her anthems
But squeezed in her legs
Like a ballad
As the chords
Came killing these speakers
And the valets
Parked our car
And we wondered
What happened to certainty
As the chill
Turned our blanket to dusk
And you asked
If I remembered the winter
And thought
We'd be together
Still.

Post–Manic Pixie Syndrome (Part 2)

I've confessed
To the fetish of intellect
As an extension
Of my own submission
To the glamour
And deliberate dominance
As unsettling
As her bookish distance
Or mystique
Of wry indifference
Such women
Are prone to exude
And the self-proclaimed
Urge of rejection
I implore
From a wealth of freckles
Or dimples
With glittering lights
Or the batting
Of mascara lashes
Shimmering from
Rooftop dawns
After concerts
On Saturday nights
And the temple
Of pagan warmth
She carries
Between her thighs

Like the vinyl gods of apathy
And ironic guilt of suitors
Who suffer
The same conditions
And addictions
To denim curves

Her ringlets
Dipped in neon
Her hair
Bundled back with sticks

And nylons
Beneath her shorts
A key of rose
Hung low
Far down her neck
To the navel
Where it stays a foreboding chain
That conditions
The entrance to tenements
Where other men
Huddle and wait
Reflecting
As if they too
Are immigrants prone to delusion
And she the shore
Of their wishes
Or landing of promised hopes
Like the Brooklyn apartment
She rents
But knows no freedom like emptiness

And the negligence
Of the many who see her
But never really know
She's real

As the male gaze
Continues to linger
As dynamite proof of her beauty
She carries in the midst
Of elusiveness
But parades
As a quirk that's chic.

Play Set

This delicate
Handblown mask
Is a face
For shattered dolls
Whose porcelain
And fragile thrones
Were concealed
Or destroyed at best
By the stronger
And lasting trinkets
That endured
Their imagined horrors
In sanctuaries
Better conceived
As a home
For missing playthings
Like stories
With settling walls
And the chipping
Of faded paints
Reminiscent
Of tiny doors
That welcome
These knocking winds
And excuse
Such outside remnants
As they shiver
From barging chills

And flee from ice
Downstairs
Where the last
Of gentle glass
Sits ominous at rest
On the hardened
Basement floors
Tucked away from vision
But lingering
Just the same
Foreboding
As existence
By the rule
Of creeping toys
Who insist
Their games are gospel
And neglect
This living vault.

Family Album

This aggregate of moments
Is an unwarranted gospel of promise
Benediction of sainted fools
Revisionist sum of halos
As canonized fixtures of age
Or captures of sacred instance
Photographic judgment
Of faces left unwilling
With women stuck at tables
As they pull from their husband's touch
A gesture of known imprisonment
An expression of cloth and wine
How it trickles with unknown tears
How it teems with flowing misuse
My scrapbooks of angry memory
My collection of enduring sacrifice
A cut and pasted penance
Where the Lord of mercy dwells
And negatives cloud His grace
And bloodlines stain the image
Of mounting cultural wrongs
Or the undoing of abusive men.

Can't Put It into Words

There was an air about that Sunday
And my thoughts amid the squalls
The way the wind had mustered
Shadows in silver daylight
And danced across the pavement
In clouds of amber leaves
And pools of saddened yellows
As the midday made its crawl
Somber as we stayed
In a hushed parade of gray
From the sidewalk to our car
With her eyes still on my feet
Focused on our pace
Like fingers to our necks
A gauge of racing beats
In cold October stillness—
So profoundly
Through that moment
I worried it would end
Not then or maybe later
But in the coming draw of distance
And beliefs of changing trends
All the missing days with parents
Or hours spent on worries
Like poems with no instance
To cite as certain death
The diatribes said to lovers
The matches in our drawers

By which we choose to hide
Instead of turning to light
Like a blazing autumn pyre
In the unexplained cause of sacrifice
Lacking any worthy grief

These memories left in parking lots
And seasons so plainly abused
Are truths I've cried in silence
But can never put into words.

At Your Door

I'll admit to
Being fearful
As you grow smaller
Near your door
As I edge up
Through these headlights
From your block
And down that street
Fessing up
To being poetic
Or arrogant
And indisposed
In the ways that
God has ruined me
Or made me
A tool for use
Anything but a partner
Or lover
And man of need
Whose servitude to your will
Is second
Only to flesh
As I watch you
Through my window
Fumbling

With your keys
Thinking
I may never see you
Once more
In that mirrored rear.

Go Get Help—I Think He Fell Down the Well

For you
I do insist
To deplete this shallow well
And through gravity
Drain its contents
To the daylight of heavy loads—
Weighted beneath the brink
In memory and in loss
Like an artifact of the bedroom
Discovered
But renowned
A force of complete resistance
A vector of sudden change
Mutual and engaged
Screaming through its pull
To acknowledge
Or claim its grievance
As it yanks the sunshine down
And smothers us in feeling
Like sentiment dark and gambled
Like seasons caught in drifts
As moments left unknown
At its bottom
A source of water
A wellspring for the weak
Complicit streams of nourishment

Conspiring forms of hope
Where you left it
But never wondered
Why it neared the gates of hell
But remained
Clear and inspired
Refreshingly unafraid
Cold to the hand of lovers
But to you
A reminder of grief

How I need her
To hold this liquid
Till I wake
From the dampened cave
And through rope
Breach deepened shadow
To the cusp of brighter aims
To the air of crisper mornings
And in freshness
Make my penance
Near the grave of circular brick
Where I work my soul entirely
And reach
An ungraspable current
Reliant on other streams
For in turn
Was a gift from God
That found me at other wells
Still thinking
Of guilty silence
Or awaiting another drink

But with hesitance
Grappling pulleys
And sensing the heft
Of my ghost
As he pushes
Beneath the barrels
And screams
From below the ground.

Enjoy Your Golden Years

They'll make you plan to see them
In the promise of hardened days
Long hours and fast commutes
Weekends lost and buried
From fear and constant motion
And conundrum of this debt
The sick and mounting convenience
Of death and paid vacations
In lungs and tired cells
In paper and absent legacy
On the bed of final penance
As you confess a weakened pulse
Knowing noise is coming black
Hoping cheer is lack of thought
Reviving you with plastics
To excuse this mournful watch
By virtue of their spitefulness
To keep you from your God
A room so filled with pretense
You'll believe they're family still
Instead of further victims
Whose turn is next to suffer
En route to the blank inevitable
As Monday comes around.

November Parkway

Have you felt
This change of weather
Across our
Wayward distance?

The landscape
Of weighted hours
Under clouds
In slighted sun?

The kind that chokes
Our safeties
Near fires as we tremble
Waiting
In thinning blankets
With the shiver
Of dwindling wills—

Like seasons
Sore from the elements
In the chill
Of nature's sleep
Chimneys bricked
And boarded
And truths from winter's glass
As we reach
The deadened grove
Of bark and sullen frost

Of balsam-scented agony
In daylight as we sleep

By which we make our turn
Round the bend
And into whiteness
Holidays bold and glistened
But beautiful
As they're missed

Now imprints
In saddest snows
Of our tales
From deep ravines
When we fall
From a moment's cliff
And into impeccable sense
That reminds us
We haven't buried
But merely just remembered
The difference
Each flake exhibits
As it shimmers
In sylvan evenings
Near the road
Where we lost our way
And wandered far from solace
Into forests
That housed our answers
Where the snow
Remained as thick.

Weekend in Her Sun

I noticed just before
How distance deemed our purpose
And method became our reason
Like the agony I'd been done
As the image I'd gone and made
Before you saw potential
To release these clenched fists
And turn my dampened palms
To face the heat of yours
As sweat came from my fingers
And mingled with each other's
To comfort the aging sun
That blistered within their crease
But never burned so far
As bright as the light you'd summon
In the prayer of a patient clasp
Swollen in delivered touch
Powered by the force of intention
You'd discovered in empty spaces
Charted with graphs of hurt

From your lips came the call of planets
The spinning of tired stars
Transmissions of hope and gravity
I feared in my failing mark
As the birth of an entire system
Became fortune by desperate science
New and old just the same

A universe unto our hearts
Bound by the matter it gave us
But sworn in the physics of bliss
As centuries could pass between us
And seasons couldn't temper fate

As if work wasn't nearly as long
As if the hours in waiting were meaningless
And absence was a slight to the heavens
Or a celestial lie at that

How these weekends build passion within us
How they narrate the inspired game
And from a mold of faith take semblance
As a droplet of rain on our car

For the weather can't hold its reaction
From a path so poignantly blazed
For a silence so whole it's maddening
In traffic so still it's fate
Or enough for storm or standard
To come between plan and orbit
For this life and our certain memory
To become what we forged in that grasp
And embellished by thoughts transcendent
Or the prospects claimed in marriage
As a birth by second chances
Of a solar and godly love.

Arden Avenue

He told me
Never get old
As I walked him to his car
But therein
Lied the figment
Of choice in our evening dark
Or light
At the end of days
From the cancer in his brain
For it was an honest
And strangely sensible
Determination of his will
To insist on working jobs
Well beyond his time of death
A season of fading sovereignty
As he staggered in the yard
And caught himself
Against the shed
Where he stumbled
And found my clasp
As I led him to the front
Where the others let me stare
At the bags
Beneath his eyes
The color of ash and coals
In circles from tested age
Disorientation
Or denial

And whatever else saw him through
As he pedaled off into night
Refusing the help we offered
But waving
As he made his turn.

Yes
It's a real solution
For those who can
Wholly believe
Or readily accept the meaning
Of value
Bargained from loss.

But the boy
Who lived inside him
Had a sickness unlike his own—
Parallel
Eerily poignant
Yet synonymous only in thought
And in permanence
A mother's burden
But through birthright
A call to neediness
That translated love
As purpose
To aid what hope was left
As his eyes
Were the revelation
That it's never an empty shell
But a semblance
Of human awareness

In suffering without cause
As he occupied
The deepest remnants
Of potential for thriving life
The steepest well of tragedy
And a proof
Of absent makers
If only to hate their existence
Or discern their baneful pride
To refute them
Altogether
And rally against their faith
To instill us
With the pain of knowing
We are alone
Helpless
But capable
Of rendering our senses hell
To convict our hopes so bold
And to confine our active truths
Of perceiving this vicious lie
As gospel
As a holy vestige
Of some sacred and grandiose nothing
That parades
As unquestioned grace
In the things
We least deserve.

Through his fits of loneliness
And grunts of unspeakable rage
I swore I could see no peace

In the kitchen as we left
But instead
A prayerful smile
Of the woman
Who held him willingly
Devotedly
And unabashedly
Nestling him ever closely
Crying
As she knew
He was all she ever had
And for him
A sole salvation
He sought as makeshift comfort
Outside the aching manner
In which his soul was prisoned
But keen
To imparting feeling
By absorbing what was given
As imbued
With precious trust
Only she and he could feel.

When I pulled off
Arden Avenue
I swore I would find my savior

A God who let this happen
To settle my score
For good.

Once more
For the sake of everyone
Who suffered
Without explanation.

To give Him
A piece of my mind
And tell Him
I was never afraid.

Ballad of the Linen Closet

This is the story
Of the girl who stayed
And knelt in my corner
When I shivered at night—
Who lay in my bed
Though I didn't deserve it,
And called out my name
When I wandered alone.

It's my tale of forgiveness
And the lust for her soul
A prayer from her work desk
And hymn toward her God.

It's the rapture in distance
And repair of her warmth
The trail of her decency
And strength of her stride—
A pathway of lifetimes
And stretch of her wishes
For the sum of one man
Whose burden was split
Of being in halves
When she knew he was whole
Sorting through pieces
And gluing each edge.

It's the impossible season
Of perpetual suns
And dawn of the hour
Whose journey toward day
Was risen excitement
From the hall to her room
Where the night grew candescent
And lifted her veil
From the swell of her bosom
From the heat of her thighs
Into faith, into intimacy
By the oath of their bed.

It's the mini vacations
And stops on the road
The losses of highways
And in-between dinners
All the hotel weddings
And wee morning visions
The light in those curtains
On the gown she had worn
How it pooled on these sheets
As she lay there in stillness
Forgetting I'm looking
As she fell fast asleep.

It's the laughable fable
Of irreconcilable difference
A formal complaint
And reactions revised.

It's everything or nothing
And a wealth of extremes
An excuse not to listen
Or an obsession of fear.

Yes, it's the tirade
And the time that I lost her
When she packed all her things
And fell from my door
Where she cried near the closet
And wept on its rags
As the blankets and towels
Knew of her losses
Wrapped her in softness
And felt her reaction
By sheer inability
To move from that floor.

It's the final text message
And twenty minutes passed
The unexpected apology
And fact she was waiting
The preemptive *we'd never*
Her assurance I knew

The makeup much later
And ever after that's coming
The one that she swore
From the second we'd met.

It's the gospel of *yeses*
And a bible of truths
Plausible miracles
Or empirical ghosts.

It's marriage and family,
A book of farewells.

It's natural but relative,
A glimpse of unknowns.

This is the poem
I knew I had written
But never admitted
I wanted to read
Or confess in its meaning
To be a lyric of yours
As a verse of infinities
That's forever in love.

Better Son

Mom and Dad
Believe when I tell you
I've written my failures
And spoke my misgivings
Pronounced all my penances
And imagined my deaths—
Not to be proud
Or gifted with graces
Accepted like age
Or tempered and kept

Pass on my legacy
Know that it's wasted
On inkwells and madmen
On anger and prose
Tell me my woman
Is safe with another
Married and happy
Far from my verse

Forget my transgressions
And learn not to fear me
And cover that wall
Where I begged with my fist.

III.
White and Blurring Lines

Act of God

I am resolute
In this distinction
That all art
Is an act of God—
Finite in its canvas
Limitless in hue
Colored
Bleeding
And broken
But perfect
In the flaw of purpose
And its creation
At the edge of stars
Garnering
Such sacred need
In the vulnerable desires
Of flesh
That are satisfied
Only in faith.

A Worthless Attempt

Breath
And this shattered
Pulse

The feeling
Of a given
Moment

Ready
To yield
At will

In waking
And prevailing
Fears

My ills
In constant
Awareness

Now tempted
By the vein
That bleeds

So dull
And achingly
Desperate

Give me
The time
Of day.

Sappho

Sappho
Had a gift
For men
Who believed in words—
She built them
A spoken womb
By which the goddess
Could grow their phrases
Birth the sacred verse
And nurture
The abstract whole
Mystery in her legs
With the dew
Of glistening sex
Moist and beckoning gospel
The source
Of the artist's prayer
Her grapes
Of hanging love
In the vineyard
Of fertile instance
And the wine
Of mingling flesh
As poetry
The blood of one
Sipped
From a woman's cup
Muse
Of eternal life.

Cosmic Light Unknown

The stars shine
In my veins
And bring forth
The aging gods
Connected on
Missing lines
Like drawings
Of a lonely child
With nothing better
To scratch
Than the measure
Of heaven's worth
In crayon
Between these worlds
His parallel human image
The color
Of celestial truth
And spectrum
Of fleeting unknowns
Like comets
In the loss
Of speech
Streaked across
Endless space.

Don't Blame the Messenger

My words
Are meant to unify
Through the chaos
Of divisive gray
Refracted
Through fogging mirrors—
The image
We can't bear
To see.

Size Never Mattered

The complexity of phrases
Relies not
On a wealth of words
Or the length
Of florid terms
Within figurative speech
But the emphasis
On captured zeitgeist
In the lightning
Of a poet's hand
And in turn
The simplicity of sentence
As the nature
Of what it relates
Or speaks
With fountain tongues
To convey
A garden of spells
In the curse
Of necessary prose
And its decorated text.

Word Bitten

I miss
The poison sting
Of a lethal
And spoken comfort
That struggled
To kill in time
Through the dose
Of written burns
Clung to
In clamping verse
And fangs
The breaching words
Where venom
Is a complacent verb
Fearing
The snarling page
As its bite
Subverts the surface
And pens
Become the kill
To administer
Fatal poison
By the phrase
That said it best.

Daily Nothing

The least
Of artists among us
Are those
Afraid to acknowledge
The secret
Of guilty cause
To express
A slanted feeling
In visions
Of purest words
And symbols
Of harbored hate—

The release
Of frantic joy
In the agony
Of broken lines
Or pictures
In rows familiar
But frightening
Seen up close
In the background
Of daily nothings
With their image
A moving cloud
And God
Their breaking sunlight
On a horizon
Not as bleak.

Always a Perfectionist (Magician)

I've mingled
With sweetest liars
Who conjure
A lasting vision
Of illusion
Grand and upheld
For the true
And straining wordsmiths
Now in padlocks
Smoke and chambers
In the mirrored
But sexy phrases
Inimitable
As smoke so transient
That billows
On center stage
In a violet plume
Of fantasy
That deceives
The eyes with drama
And ears
Assaulted by melody
To bemuse
That begging crowd
And release
This brave assistant
To turn her curves
To worship

Trading
Mystique for clarity
As she binges
On the high of applause
All for the effort of faking
And in lust
The thrill of creating
What terms
Are quite endearing
As the magic
Of a perfect escape.

Gnosis

They tell me
God is a needle
That threads
A lasting wound
Who seals
A blistered gash
On the souls
Of indentured men—

But religion
Isn't a system
Or a bartered
Notion of grace

It's a god
Unto itself

A star
Unlikely to wander

And always
A personal truth

Which like people
Eventually fades.

True and Just

Love
That's true and just
Is the kind where
You stay afraid
And stifle
The red in your eyes
From responding
To yes in the dark
And crying
From a need so dirtied
Battered
Maintaining a semblance
Of rivers
Sustaining such motives
As they flow like rapids
So rough
Cresting
At the peak of abandon
Outward
In furious arches
And curve
Like a bend
Into nothing
To move from the danger
That splits

As it mangles
Both faces distinctly
From the cascade
Of emptying waters
Like tears
Of unyielding disaster
That turn into hurt
As they land.

Retrospective (Integer)

In hindsight
We are all irreparable
Like a vector
Of mangled ambition
Careening on
A dotted road
Checkered like
Living graphs
And marred
By skidding lines
Mistaken for
A one-way curve
On an angle
From how
To when

An axis
Of concave glass
Measured
In certain points
But mistaken
For empirical truth
That's shattered
Toward the break
Of infinity

But nearly
Reaches
Its limit
Without ever
Accepting the terms
Of a resolute
And positive integer
Now absolute
From the death
Of its value
As erased
By the pencil
Of God.

Checkerboard

Anticipate
The changing turns
As we approach
A rule of kings—

I want you
To remember games
Because law
Is a lasting challenge
That exceeds
The age of children
And crushes
All men who persist
Beyond the need
For worthiness
Or desire
To make due with flaws
Or accept
The subjective happiness
Of removing
All streaks of color
Stripped
Like fun from pieces
And replaced
With a painted wood
On boards
Without proper sanding
Splinters

Like stakes at their edge
No grays
Just black-and-white emptiness
Good
Or evil
Or nothing
As they abuse
The unknowing player
In a move
They never desire
Or anticipate
Like sudden jumps
Like the task
To remove and reach
The point
That's farthest from home
And dethrone
An equal man
By establishing
Superior feats
Through shattering
A lasting dream
Or humble plot
That he's settled
As a persistent ground
Of his own.

This gamble
Of cutthroat skill
That neglects
The space between
And forces

Belief on the other
Insists upon
The hand of business
And swells
For competitive kills
As we endure
In a test of morals—
How we all fail
By maintaining purpose
Without ever
Having a choice.

Robin's Nest (Never You)

It's the hand
Of cryptic divinity
And the humor
Of cosmic truths
That all such
Laughing matters
Be the product
Of grinning martyrs
And impermanence
Their waving legacy
Twisted
From the highest canopy
And woven
In brightest fibers
From the scraps
Of collective ills
Or the cruelty
Of other beasts
Filtered through
Bearded genius
But carried
On wayward drifts
As the burdens
In mounting squalls
Become rays
Of festered radiance
Pooled in
The palm of morning

Like a cupped
And sweeping gesture
Pointing
To existing heavens
In the clouds
By the cue of mirth
For all animals
But this bird
And its ability
To sing regardless
Of acknowledgment
Of birthing dawns
And the herald
Of expected suns
It created
And allowed for us
But kept
So little alone
And allotted
What's left to the rest
As it chirped
To the final daybreak
And left these eggs
Of gleefulness
Spotted blue
In the grandest tree
But fallen so far
From melody
As the branch
Gave way beneath
And the forest
Forever wept

Knowing Robin
Would never nest
Anymore
In its fleeting midst.

New Face

Through fear
And unfiltered agony
Must I dictate
Unspeakable gospel
To determine
The fount of grief
In a wellspring
Of faithful cause
As I bear
This stubborn challenge
Of stricken
And agitated belief
That's fallen
So far from saintliness
But professes
How the growth of seasons
And the shedding
Of dying leaves
Is an autumn
Of coming heavens
In the purifying
Chill of winter
And the will
Of familiar persons
So necessary
In their zeal
Is the ideal
Of reaping harvests

To the delight
Of nature's tendency
To spark hope
In innocent acts
Or the eyes
Of knowing beasts
That admit
To the bliss of instinct
And elicit
Compliant purity
In the moment
We cannot seize
But merely
Taste in vain
Optimistic
As fallen gods
Or religion
Of changing face
That redeems
Our inner fiend.

Rail Yard (The Switchman)

There's a switchman
In our midst
Who awaits
The uncommon signals
And triggers
Unruly motions
As the iron
Rains his truths
And judges
Remembered tracks
In the stakes
Of risking being
For the glory
Of enduring steel
Or the testament
Of failing hubris

The boxcar
And freighted testaments
Of the privileged
And dining no
Trivial
As their answer
In the breath
Of an empty soot
Blackened
Like billowing ash
As intellect

Or inspired coal
A purposeful
Lack of destiny
Whimsy
In the face of fate
A steam
Whose boasted engine
Is a gamble
Of fearful sorts
Striking laughter
In the heart of God
And roars
Near quivering lips
In the trip
From purposeful stations
To the peace
Of darkened country
Or candles
Of waking valleys
Rejecting
The call of changes
As they turn
Their ear in sleepiness
Or hear
The eternal gears
Of metals
In need of phantoms
For their final
And silent tour
Behind
Such pampered walls
And the destined flight

Of tourists
Who'll listen
For that very hiss
Just to ponder
Restoration
In ignorance
As they forget
The unflinching switchman's gaze
Who looked
From his dreaded days
To a cause
Of another's dream
And valued
The folly of science
So that irony
Willed his lantern
In that last
And attempted gesture
Wasn't heaven
Or a promise of hell
But a message
From charging behemoths
That vengeance
Is a gift of discipline
And simplicity
A forgotten virtue
Like the age
Where it all made sense
And value
Wasn't crowded ethics
Or meaning
His rusted wisdom

Just as that
Wandering echo
Carried on
Through the rail yard
Alone.

Almost Lost the War

Call it
Acquired jadedness
Or the buildup
Of passing age
Like taut
And demanding layers
Sagging from
Sweating bullets
Skin of tired years
Sunken
With pointed curves
And dry marks
Blush from tears
As the cracks
Uphold their reasons
For the splitting
Of beloved parts
Or divide
Of accepted notions
We've faintly
Acknowledged as truthfulness
Or otherwise
A wealth of presumptions
In the prose
Of unruly nothings
In the stretches
Of yellow acres
Wastelands

Of hollow visions
Or the memory
Of zealous guns
Who maintained
Their will in trenches
And spoke
For imprisoned villains
In the battery
Of God's last testament
With casings
And artillery shells
The faithfulness
Of drowning armadas
The steel
Of empowered morals
And ethics
Of attempted grenades
Whose burst
Was a word in edgewise
As it smoldered
Near the hole
We call permanence
And died
From a wounded religion
Convincing
Enough to be cruelness
Like the impostor
Of a polished lord
With medals
A sword
And mask
To filter the chemical skeptics

And raid
The last of libraries
As the warfare
Grows airborne and wide
The longer
We bide our hours
And grieve
With desperate conviction
In the time
Of imagined victories
Where the conquest
Is merely stalled
And the imperative
Remains indecent
At the hands
Of recycled heroes
And the lovers
Abandoned in sewers
As makeshift
And glorious homes—
Righteous
In their bloodied annex
Where warmth
Is a body up close
And escape
Is the fearful witness
Kissing
The first of the saved
Predicting
The ache of their verse
And poetry
Suffering silence

As believers
Wreak havoc above them
And the cynics
Bear witness below.

Commitment

For you I would
Beg to differ
With anything less than gold
And argue to great extents
With the standard of settled silver
If it meant securing the melody
Of your heartbeat in a jar

Your smile under a veil
Your kiss like a plume of smoke

A ready stove of commitment
An ashen shade of grace

From which you create bronze
And cast it in gilded hopes
Only to learn this forge
Was as capable as stars
In the birth of priceless cinders
That ember for eternal halves
That bridge the darkness of loss
And sparkle across the gap
Lonely but predestined
Balanced as the abyss
As certain as their glow
In search for solid matter
That brought them into orbit
And orchestrated cause

A form of impassioned movement
As dictated by their nature
Just as my lust for metals
Brought me to hidden stones
A gem I'd sought in ruins
A diamond in fallen mines
As I swear to polish your edge
And savor your loving glimmer
Each time I acknowledge the richness
Of a woman of rarest finds.

Silk Flowers

From the ground
Comes a weed
As it breaks the satin ash
Through textile
And potted soil
From woven
And synthetic earth

Its stem like rising truth
In the midst
Of threaded buds
Counterfeit
Unashamed
This manufactured rose

Now tested by that vine
As it blooms a greener herb
Unwanted
But original
Organic
Uncontrolled

A sleight by the hand of God
As the gardener reaps his sin
At the cost of fabrication
Artificial as our will

To seek beauty in its ills
And improve
Upon perfection
That is the growth of unwanted grass
Like all things
Made from man

As we near
The summer's end
And reach
For autumn spoils
From the cloth
Of sprouted rags
And harvests
With bitter fruits.

They Wear T-Shirts

As I see them in the shops
By the plaza
Near their cars
There is something
Quite unnerving
In the way they
Wear their clothes
And don such fitted sweaters
Sporting
A touted catchphrase
Like "Love"
Below their necks
Or "Freedom"
Near their chests
A message so recycled
And slogans of easy changes
Such expression
Upsets nothing
But their fingers sore
From bags

How interesting
Rebellion
Is a powerful form
Of retail.

How unbecoming
Of a generation
That revolution
Is a marketed brand.

Transit Lane

We all ride
To seek some distance
In the stretch
That defines our own—
A headlight bright
In waiting
For the night to change its reason
And like crystal
Refract its dusk
As we travel
On faulty promise
By asphalt and scripted faults
Beaming through peaking cracks
Like gloss
In darkened prisms
Like veins
Of pebbled ruin
And through seasons scraping ash
Escaping the widening hour
An abyss
Of clouded Sundays
Awaiting the evening rains
As we thirst
For final holidays
In the nothing
Of a forward glance
Toward passengers barely chosen
In vehicles leased on faith

In the hopes of some vacation
Commuting on Monday trains
Toward the daylight
In our ironies
Of believing we'd come so close
Or had witnessed
From missing stations
As the farthest thing from home.

Waiting Area

Silence
Is full acknowledgment
Of no greater form of grieving

As a contract
Of allowed bereavement
And consensus of final cost
To mourn the loss of feeling
To administer a suited ends
Of irony at its best
Of pretense at its worst
And through gesture
Seize its hour
As our breath betrays this stance
And by need
Expire timidly
Like billows in lighted dark—
To linger
Like air from heaving
And settle on tired lungs
From the efficiency
Of being useless
And the expenditure
Of needless smoke.

What matters
Is not the intake
But the expelling
Of equal means.

IV.
This Blank and Frozen Slate

Flew the Coop

Under better skies
I believed
In the truth
Of a willing God

But despite
This desperate climate
My faith
Is a daring wing
Like the flutter
Of a fleeting bird
Beneath bigger
And lonelier clouds
That soars
As courageous virtue
Where the weather
Is perpetually glum.

A Series of Dots

Here's to looking at you
From behind
The brush's perception
On the easel
Of lingering thought
Or the streak
Of lasting feeling
And distance
In summer color
As it fractures
The pastel features
Of moments
Turned to grace
As you tilt your head
Indefinitely
While the sun
Refracts its glimmer
Into instants
Of perpetual glow
Knowing
This pensive frown
Is a moment
Explicitly captured
Like the eternal
And abstract flower
Of an Impressionist

Recalling a garden
Only now
An image of womanhood
So evocative
So tacitly stated
In emotion
And evening sunshine
Palette of forever obsession
As she muses
Her state of beauty
While perfection
Loses its touch
And the painting
Remains a window
But the love
Is far removed
And that seat
Is an empty memory
A reminder
Of vivid reality
And the stunning nature
Of loss
As it hangs
From the thread of a hook.

Maya

If you imagine the hardest joy
In the sanctity of life
You've barely foreseen
The heaven
Of her God
And giver of gifts—
The keeper
Of moving words
The pusher
Of spoken worlds
And poet
Of conjured angels
Who dwelled among hateful men
But became
A gentle teacher
And prophet of risen terms
Graceful
Inviting
And warm
With her phrase the majestic legacy
This love a lasting cause
To withstand
Denounce
And encompass
A gospel of breathing history
And art

An extension of hands
To those in need of belief
Her children
At the foot of their mother
Listening
Clinging
Appreciating
The wisest of imparted speech.

Young and Naive

Maybe it's my flaw
That I dream in a different key
And perceive
Surrounding bodies
As a spectrum of moving hues
Because the minute
They lose all color
I admit to the loss of self
And submit to a faithless rage
That is born
Of this burdensome lie

Conceived in expectation
And executed like law:

Where is the sense of God
In this roundabout
Of endless work
And the labor of broken saints
Whose souls are contrived
In purpose?

I prefer
The indefinite impulse
Of who and what
We are—
Creatures innately human
Inquiring within ourselves

For the answer
In faulted stars
And discovering
The sun within
Not the chill
Of ample funds
Or the shiver
Of silent desks
Eight-hour liturgies of death—
Impermanent as they are—
Leading to corrupted hearts
And the finality
Of senseless choice.

It is not the plight of nature
For us to toil so.

We ruined
Ransacked
And deviated
From the beat of our rhythmic pulse
Betrayed the needs of flesh
Desecrated
The gift of art.

When will we
Measure our neighbor
Not by their use or status
But the echo
Of gospel within
And the size of tear-stained murals
Painted in demand for unity

Compassion
Vision
And love?

Each day
I go to work
I die a little more
Inside.

And not for
Reasons unknown
But because
We're all wasting together

And fading
Into obscurity
From heaven
In the here and now.

Woman of the Sky

She is a spectrum
Of attractive doubts
And a gift
Of the falling sun
As a daughter
Of thundering judgment
Not far
From beloved earth
Or rays
Of the burning curve
That climb
This maddening distance
To encompass
The heat of her heart
As the dawn
Grows dim from waiting
And the dusk
Awaits her tryst
As a final
And passionate cycle
For the exchange
Of moonlit hours
Within cause
Of continuous day.

A kiss now
Of the celestial woman
Who beams
From the heavens like fire
And promises
Another sunrise
Through worship
We long to uphold.

Toujours

This resplendent curve
Is a sumptuous
But trifling detail
Of a dancer
Whose tune is meddlesome
As her stance
And pointed affair
That's always
A spot at the bar
Constantly
Outlined in mirrors
And fading
Like white chalk in spotlight
Where the dust settles lithely
Underfoot
As she shudders
Near the peak of elegance
And in climax
Becomes a frame of cinema

Noir
Edgy
And visual

A carnal yet eloquent kiss

This starlet
Of unconscious scandal
Arousing
Beneath burdens of shadow
Like instinct
Gambled but certain
Trembling
Forever poised.

Mother of Exploration

Notice
The sheltering voice
As she reaches
With open fingers
And cradles
The curve of his neck
With posture
And sensitive grace
Like a dancing
Liturgy of hands
In the heave
Of careening decks
Before leaning
Above closing eyelids
And caressing
The pinch of his cheeks
Just as the hull gives way
Nuzzling
The perch of his nose
As the heaviness
Rocks from storms
And waves
Bring him closer to bliss
As she kisses
The crack of his lips
With rain
On such sandy shores
And relieves famine

In the drought of hearts
From the starving needs
Of natives
Whose presence
In the queen of courtship
Begs an audience
With bipolar gods
Whose tricks
Are snide but regal
As they ring across
Kingdoms of men
And are fulfilled
By the courage of women
Whose sea
Is their destined pathway
In expedition
Of romantic discovery
On to continents
Virgin and due.

A Night Away

Let this be
Our tethered rope
With burning ends
And matches used

Our fondest silence
And nervous minds
On broken cords
Or roaming calls

These yearning hearts
Are missing evidence
Of daylight texts
And summer spells

We bathe in dreams
We set suspicions

I'm counting reasons
You wish them real

Without an answer
Lacking empathy

I know I can't
You show me how:

Come back soon
Come back whole
Come back naked
Come back loved

How I spend
Your night away
In listing grief
Through staggered verse
Evident fears
Or anxious sleep
And playing God
With desperate words

A set of shadows
You dispel in truth
To erect in memory
Which fails me now.

Fresh Start

The gift
Is not a flower
But a stem
To hold its beauty

The same
Can be said of people
Who nurture
The will of others

And inspire
The breath of passion
By sustaining
Roots in soil
And imbuing
The soul with rainfall
To savor
The worth of suns
That inevitably
Melt our winter
Toward the promise
Of better seasons
From spring
To fertile summer
And autumn
Lush with grain

Know this
Like a farmer
And prepare
For certain harvest
By sowing
Seeds of goodness
In each action
Rich like dirt.

Village Winter

The golden bells
Of aging churches
Tired summits
And whitened Alps
Are a tolling phase
In your withered voice
And a touch of brass
Like tightening nerves
By the smack of tin
Against this wall
Of amber brick
In narrow streets
And solemn breath
In tongues of frost
Near frigid branches
Where the widow mourns
In fading billows
Beneath the pines
Under creaking roofs
Of warmer bars
For younger times
And the lust of many
Not etched in stone
But buried in snow.

Joyce at One a.m.

I fear most
The act of writing
And volumes
Of leather-bound heroes
Whose mythic
And aging promise
Is a deceased
Mosaic of figments
That settle like
Dusty gales
Once the wind
Has brought them justice
And in hindsight
Served its vision
Like an umbrella
Obscuring their motto

As these moments
Are cause for attention
And readers
The pretense of value
Attributed
To glaring errors
On behalf
Of begging legends
Whose names
Are not their terms
But coin

The phrase of enmity
That embitters
A whole of teachers
And enlivens
A set of artists
To denounce
Their colored portraits
As a copy
Of unparalleled negatives
Whose monochrome truth
Was inimitable
And tales of bohemia
Invincible
As the expected
Hatred of self
From the smear
Of lasting oils
And the dabs
Of haunting frescos
Inevitable
As she walks
A muse from page to hourglass
Tears
From thighs to bottles
As it rings
Like solemn indemnity
Tolling the brass of this hour
Where his heart
Is unwritten jealousy
And the prose
Is refined by spite
As the tongue

Curls back on his passion
To speak
For the love of her

Like the sex
Of a spoken God
Whose name
Is the perfect verb
She can never
Hope to achieve
But merely
Indirectly inspire

As the greats
And history expire
Subside
In the falling night
And Joyce
Is the blanket of knowledge
Reminiscent
Of his image of snow
As the poet gleams
In his dreaming
Of forever
Imbued in his tries
To emulate
The perpetual drinkers
Stars
And tawdry losses

And ravers
Of ambiguous decades
In the motion
Of passing sleep

And constellations
Behind his eyes
Stringing
Like a verse too long
Unconsciously
Begging confusion
To worry him
Into peace.

Timekeeper

Scholars
Have spent idle centuries
Distilling
Their raw ideals
To an equation
Of sudden causes
And descriptions
On the basis of action

Like a timepiece
Sworn to its measure
But subject
To inaccurate gears
As the means
Of procuring freedom
Is left
To the bottomless quill
Of madmen
Set on answers
With a theory
Of falsehoods at hand
And circles
With senseless notions
That are methods
For going insane.

It pains me
To see how knowledge

And the pursuit
Of satisfaction
Has become
A crusade of cowards
Convinced
Their viewpoint is deft—
Rationalized
By begging soldiers
Who binge
So efficiently on sustenance
In the dust
Of drying tomes
And the sills
Of broken histories

Like a blackened
Window to pleasures
Of the cerebral
And anxious minds
That fear
The written destinies
Of failure
In their smoking hubris
And truth
In writhing convention
In the perversion
Of convincing fallacies
That have made
This conundrum worse
Through the glass
Of translucent hopes
Or belief

That life is potential
To solving
For the massive "X"
We know
Is just false religion
Dictated
By the silent timekeeper
Whose game
Is allowing conjecture
By the elite
Ensnared in its lie

Some things
Just have to go *tick*
Before the bomb is revealed
A dud
Or perhaps maybe something
Like the maniacs
Always said
It would.

Why It Goes Unsaid

Insist upon
The clearing of airs
And acknowledgment
Of open veins
By disclosure of covered nooses
Tied readily
Beneath our clothes
Or the rigid
And angled dagger
Kept hidden in quivering hands
As our sleeve
Conceals this weapon
Each day of rampant chores
And the runaway ills
Of progress
As we cope with settled acceptance
Of the notion
We're damaged goods
To affirm the gentle valiance
Of confessing
To belief in assistance
Even from strangers' hands
Whose blood runs warmer still
And pulses
In prayerful rhythms
As the silenced God of charity
Whom we neglect
In daily vengeance

And forget
In abundant bread
As catered as we remain
But discontent
With how we're placed
And the fact
That it can't be shared
Across a blistering boundary
And fractured set of nations
And standards
Impoverished and weak
As the souls who mandate evil
In the tombs
Of proper smiles
Or conflict deemed necessity
To negate a social risk
Dictate a deck of cards
And choose the most valued player
As the best of us rescind our promise
Or the rest of them cower in loss
Undignified
And softly spoken
Quiet or unexpected
Noble as their death
Or hatred toward themselves
Without anyone ever knowing
'Cause the climate
Is ripe for rain
And unwelcome
Of coming suns
Just beyond their reach.

Reader

The sin
Of telling stories
Is we wish them
To be true
As the stilted
World of fiction
Is an effigy
Of control—

From the hand
Of fickle genius
Or the heart
Of impassioned cynics
Arrested
With their inks
And shackled
To their thoughts
Ideals
Of sudden weakness
Remnants
Of failed attempts
Their cross
Of deliberate saviors
And countermeasure
By conjecture

A compendium
Of broken players

Deemed iconic
In their flaws
Written
For delinquent dreamers
In their quest
To become symbolic
And seek meaning
Where there is little
To mine worth
Where there is only feeling
Or nothing
But mirrored neuroses
In the frivolous
Guise of words.

Source

Would you believe me
If I told you
Of the love of the eternal muse
And alms of her given lyrics
The melody of her rhyme
Divinity of her speech
Catastrophe of her grace
And comedy on her heels
In the wake of treaded heavens
Or paths of inspired hells
By virtues of her crown
And the flowers of her touch
For all those left unmoved
By the mountains she can push
Or men she's turned immortal
By thrusting them from cliffs
And leaping into destinies
On the faith of batted eyes
Or hair of golden threads
Like the aroma from her sex
As intimate as her speech
From the well of forbidden phrase
Or graze of tangled flesh
And light in distant verse
She's dangled from her influence
A mirror to the heart of God

The seed of written apostles
Birthed in a sainted womb
And bestowed like living truth
This child of poetic agony
This babe of suffered miracles.

A Type of Poetic Justice

To bear witness
Or account for poetry
Is to instigate
The victim of difference
And attest
To its plague of penitence
As a spoken
And admired insolence
By which
The vicarious charm
Or feverish swell of confidence
Is a dangling hook of exposures
Disclosed
In adolescent wishes
But denied
Like boyish appeal
As addiction
As rightful ineptitude
Imagined as
Famed dependence
Weighted
On the heels of instants
The turns of
Golden phrases
Nouns of
Hellish willingness

Syllables of
Skillful nothings
To plead in
Written histories
And run from
Compiled texts
All testimonies
Unfit for gospel
Or tragedies
Coined in vengeance
Of the loving
And disparaged remnants
Accosted
By romantic vagrants
And seekers
Of criminal verbs
Who wander
In spite of loneliness
Who tremble
For the coming muse.

Point of Entry

I can pinpoint
The quoted second
I expected
Myself to change
And the delivery
Of its minute
As the second hand
Stood its gauge
And rested in
Firm resistance
Like a moment
With hope to pardon
In anticipation
Of such arrogance
And eloquence
All at once
By which I was
Sworn to permanence
As the vested
Power of words
Ticking away at ends
By which I increase my age
And in measure
Abide by rules
Transfixed by breaking laws
As I educate

My riled stance
To propel my distance forward
Farther
And carried onward
As the militant root of traditions
I've potted
And poured to a boil
The way I flow like liquid
The way dreams
Shiver and spill
Evaporate
And turn from heat
All the workdays
And prime endeavors
Wasted in private rains
From the climate
Of storming minds
I've broken by walking laziness
Like shoes
On sandy roads
Stretched by their casual willingness
To mold
To the wearer's fit
And detach
Their leathery lace
From strides
To release this soul
Or sole beneath its print
From hindering open paths
By the strangled and quitted strut

Admired
By the village noose
Unsettled
As the man who stayed
Sentenced
To easy punishment
By a death
He called his own

Consider it
A point of entry
My detached
And impassioned speech
By the unwavering
Course of sorrows
I've measured
Sublime and captive
Unsure
Unheard
Not reticent
But flavored in rainbow paint
As the choice perversion of terms
In the outspoken
Verbs of color
I've drowned
In meaningless verse
But feared
Like castrated meaning
Imbued from a sense of self
Or appointed

In frantic haste
The unbending will of libido
The stifling
Grossness of ease
Unabashed
And unconscious
But favored
So mockingly splendid
In the richness
Of unbridled truth
Or expression
Set out to pasture
That is far
From wasted effort
In making myself
A name.

Rest Assured

The mountains
We push in faithfulness
Are feats not far from God
As strength
Is not the mover
But the changing hearts of man
That pry
With great conviction
As testament to such beliefs
And rattle
With sudden tremors
To foil the firmest ground
Unsteady with wanton idols
Or the seismic rift of words
Language
And foreign cultures
Or currency built on hate
As examples
True and wounded
Of divinity and harshest graces
The willingness to conform
And woven love unmeshed
By the spindle
Whose time is sacred
And borrowed
From threads of saints
Or angels
Like knitted shepherds

Guardians of inner night
Vigilant
Ever stoic
Protective of their flock
And in reason
A sacred argument
To existence
Meant as hours
Or the distance
Of needy converts
In the watchful eye
Of Christ.

Composition

In the coldest wind
At harshest instants
From the earliest hour
To the latest breath
I want this song
To be your drummer
A distance bridged
A promise kept
Some secret known
Or kindled prayer
A silent flame
And spoken whole
Your warm reminder
Your lost confession
A softest shield
And protective note
An inner tempo
Of blindest melody
A genius symphony
Of truths untold
To propel your heart
And conduct its pulse
To where it stays
In restless harmony
And in ballads wait
But in music plays
Like true love grows
By the waltz of roses

And swell of cheeks
Red from feeling
Clipped in dance
Arranged in kisses
And displayed through trust
By which I swear
To beg your voice
In dual movement
A lifelong concerto
A marriage that
God's chorus lifts
In eternity raises
And through children's chatter
Compose our reasons
Depicts our souls
And write our fate.

V.
Skating across the Cracks

Outpatient Therapy

I write
To become
The disaster
I've always been
In my head.

Made an Attempt

By virtue
Of broken days
I savored
The lasting hours

In hindsight
I gathered fortunes
On the collapse
Of a raging sun.

Can't Say You Didn't

I fight
Like there is
Nothing left
Because
Tomorrow
That's always
The case.

Truth Hurts

There's nothing
In this verse
But the glass
Of a shattered man
And a point
Of jagged talent
I'm convinced
Will be my end.

Hasty Decision

Nothing short
Of spontaneous
Is worth
Any effort
Given.

Kept to Oneself

I'm alive
In broken afterthoughts
When alone
And scrounging
For warmth

Like images
Cut from memory
As this film reel
Fades to black

With photographs
In grayscale filters
Strewn as shadows
Deliberate

Across pictures
Imagined by emptiness
Cutting scenes
From the bedroom floor.

Two Sides

The best lies
Are deeply personal
And written in
Poetic truth.

Contrived

Drivel
Is the profound intuition
Of knowing one's phrase
Has failed.

Embellished

I've lost my voice
So often
It barely even matters
I speak
Or attempt
To reclaim this word
That refuses to become
One sentence
But stays
A perpetual calling
Like lifetimes
Embellished in ink.

OCD

Everything
Is somehow
Crooked
Or nearly
A distance
Apart.

Borderline

I fear as though
I may be distant
But rage
Says I'm closer
Than most
Like a feeling
Unready
To be spoken
Or a tool
That's wedged
Between souls—

Sometimes
The spell is buoyant
Other times
It's a capsized boat

Still
I believe in meaning
Despite
What has swallowed me
Whole.

Bad Couple of Weeks

Nothing
Speaks the plight
Of an amateur
Like the lack
Of feeling
In words.

Says a Lot about Me

The happier
I've come to feel
The less I'm able
To write.

Contract

If I write
For recompense
There is nothing left
To these words
But a sad
Imagined meaning
Of marketable
Soulless trash
That removes
The sacred feeling
Of sentiment
Straight from the gut.

Indulgence

If God is overlooked
There is no choice
But to call it
Art.

Author's Rope

Writing is
An effective measure
And swinging gauge
Of a ruined life—
It is a length of letters,
And a knot of poems
A hanging angel
In a killer mob
By lengthy ropes
That leave them dangling
With beloved devils
Who enraged them all.

Back and Forth

For the ills
We wish on others
So do we
Enrich our deaths
And in oblivion
Heed our debts
A little bit
At a clip

Like a load
Of empty shells
Or just by
Another inch
Of the noose
To which we all aspire
And swing
When most deserved.

Cup of Coffee

After each day
Solemnly waking
To attend to my
Morning illness

I am convinced
And blissfully confident
In this bitter
And cloudy poison
That nihilism
Isn't far
From reality
And nothingness
Is this swallowed
Cup.

Self-Employed (Salary)

My contingency is death
Or life on brighter mornings
Depending how I wake
Or if circumstance permits
To allow me base securities
That a grown man barely has
Or shouldn't if he works
For minimum cost of dreams.

Man of Many Words

I don't have
Any talents
But the gall
To admit
To feeling

Or the verbosity
Of being wrong
In a lengthy
Explanation.

Burden

What terms
I would endure
If it means
An echoed phrase
A legacy of verbs
Or at least
A written eternity.

Pharisee

How unsteady
The honest man
Whose truth
Is his brick of faith
And hope
A cemented logic
Piled high on
Anxious minds
Like his claim
Of just desserts
Or taxes
Obliged and sought
Rhetoric
His stoic platform
But hypocrisy
Saving grace

Sturdy as
Knotted wicker

Resilient
As human waste.

Feigning Confidence

How must I
Be content
By any standard
Except my own?

How would I
Value ambition
If daylight
Was risen indifference?

No Apologies

As certain
As tomorrow
More contrived
Than the will of God
I anticipate
The coming words
Of egregious
And cloudy dawns
But only
If the nerve persists
Or rains

Draw anxious blood
And spilled
This relentless vein
Upon the ignorance
Of settled men.

Perpetual

Subjectivity
And ambiguity
Are beautiful until you learn
Morality forever teeters
On the cusp
Of night and day
Straddling
Chosen dusk
But leaning
Ever closer
In the direction
Of decisive dawn
Or certainty once defined
As catalyst
Of a cause
Or model
As perfect sin.

Can't Win 'Em All

If verses
Were considered riches
I'd be far too spoiled
To know
How often
Their weight stayed golden
How easily
Such wealth was spent.

Here Comes the End

Perhaps I'll garnish
My sorrows
In an amended means
Of diligence
If it entails
A cleansing of image
And functioning
As a wordless lip
Insistent
As the faulty silence

That renders my voice
As useless
To reason this truth
As voided
And in holiness
Hold my tongue—

For verbs
As language knows
Often betray
The bravest sentence
By voices intent
On capturing
The action
Of a perfect phrase

An inkling
As I labor
To write these terms
In spite

And shudder
From innate tendency
To acknowledge
Their spoken chill.

Advice to My Father

Every single
One of us
Is born
Into an instance
Of pain

Learn this
And complain
In empathy

Perhaps then
You will see
The difference.

Fleeting Thought

The fact
Of the matter is
She never
Really left.

Sour Grapes

Creation drives
The hardest bargain
Which sees us building
Bigger walls

For it is difference
That gives us
Meaning

But love
That makes it
Lethal.

Chewed Out

I've needled and sawed
This grain
With a tooth
That's chipped its edge
From fair and honest hungers
But convinced
Of better pangs
In fangs of pearly diamond
With whites of splintered jaws

And bitten
By the hand that feeds
In night
When the grind persists
To spite what truth
Was left
In the privilege
Of an open mouth.

All the Trouble I'd Save

From the minute
We are born
They need to
Pull the plug.

Give Thanks

Humanity has
And always will be
A crime unto
Its self—
A simple whimper
And whispered breath
Of decaying triumph
In senseless loss.

Last-Ditch Effort

Write them
A lonely suicide
To read on their way
To work
And somehow
The world will love you
For confessing
You played that part

But hold them up
A mirror
To show that they're just
As guilty

And they'll squirm
In nervous silence
To avoid each other's eyes

By closing that page
In protest
Or ignoring
Your desperate letter

Knowing they caused
This instance
By laughing it off
As truth.

Chokehold

If you want to see
Injustice
Then just stand
On the nearest
Corner.

Some Reason, Some Season

Bless
The Child

But save
The receipt.

Acknowledgments

I owe the following people a special debt of gratitude and extend my sincerest thanks for making this compilation come to fruition with consummate excellence through unwavering dedication:

Andrew E. Lisanti III, my cousin and confidant, who inspires me on every level with his immense artistic talents and enduring work ethic. Our journeys and experiences together mean the world to me, and I look forward to whatever adventures await us as long as we can share them. His photographic vision and contributions are uncanny, and I am eager and proud to showcase them alongside my poetry.

My mother and father, Linda and Dominick Pigno, who are the foundations upon which I lay my entire life. Every single word is owed to their unconditional love.

All of my family, friends, and mentors who, through the years, have guided me to this point. Without them, I'd be nothing.

About the Author

Jonathan D. Pigno was raised in Staten Island, New York. Pigno graduated from Wagner College and has always had a love of the written word. His work has appeared in *Five 2 One* magazine, *Vine Leaves Literary Journal*, *Asbury Pulp*, *365 Tomorrows*, *INdulge* magazine, *SI View*, *Taste* magazine, and the *Staten Island Advance*.

When he isn't writing, Pigno enjoys watching movies, reading comic books, playing video games, and indulging in his passion for pop culture. For more information about his writing, he invites you to visit his website, www.jonathanpigno.com.

www.ingramcontent.com/pod-product-compliance
Lightning Source LLC
LaVergne TN
LVHW021119080426
835510LV00012B/1749